D0520571

Spiders, Worms, and Bugs, Oh My!

Copyright 2009 (Third Edition)   Sopris West Educational Services. All rights reserved.

Read Well is a registered trademark of Sopris West Educational Services.

No portion of this work may be reproduced or transmitted
in any form or by any means, electronic or mechanical,
including photocopying or recording, or by any information
storage and retrieval system, without the express written
permission of the publisher.

ISBN 10-Digit: 1-59318-860-9

ISBN 13-Digit: 978-1-59318-860-3

12 11 10 09   3 4 5 6

Printed in the United States of America

Published and Distributed by

Sopris West™
EDUCATIONAL SERVICES

A Cambium Learning Company

4093 Specialty Place • Longmont, CO 80504 • (303) 651-2829
www.sopriswest.com

JDE 148929

TABLE OF CONTENTS
THE BABY BEEBEE BIRD cover courtesy of HarperCollins Children's Books.

Unit 7

PHOTO CREDITS
3, 11: ©Fotolia/Ismael Montero. 4, Clockwise from top right: ©istockphoto.com/Milo
Sluz; ©istockphoto.com/Arlindo Silva; ©Kai's Power Photos; ©istockphoto.com/Geotrac;
©istockphoto.com/Sergey Zholudov. 5: ©istockphoto.com/Tomasz Resiak. 6: ©Photodisc/
Punchstock. 7: ©istockphoto.com/Gavin MacVicar. 8: ©istockphoto.com/Leonid Smirnov.
9: ©istockphoto.com/Edyta Cholch-Cisowska. 10: ©DigitalVision. 12: ©istockphoto.
com/Tomasz Resiak. 13, Clockwise from top left: ©istockphoto.com/Caitrione Dwyer;
©Designpics.com/Punchstock, ©Royalty-Free/Corbis. 14: top, ©Jupiter Images; bottom,
©istockphoto.com/Michel Mory.

ILLUSTRATION CREDITS
Lap Book illustrations: Bobbi Shupe

Unit 8

ILLUSTRATION CREDITS
Lap Book illustrations: Larry Nolte

Unit 9

ILLUSTRATION CREDITS
Lap Book illustrations: Stacey Schuett

Spiders, Worms, and Bugs, Oh My!

Lap Book 3

UNITS 7 • 8 • 9

READ WELL

Sopris West Educational Services

Spiders, Worms, and Bugs, Oh My!

Students explore the fascinating world of spiders, worms, and insects, sing a song of wiggly-jiggly worms, and make their own zoo animal masks.

Eric Carle · The Very Busy Spider

Related Literature

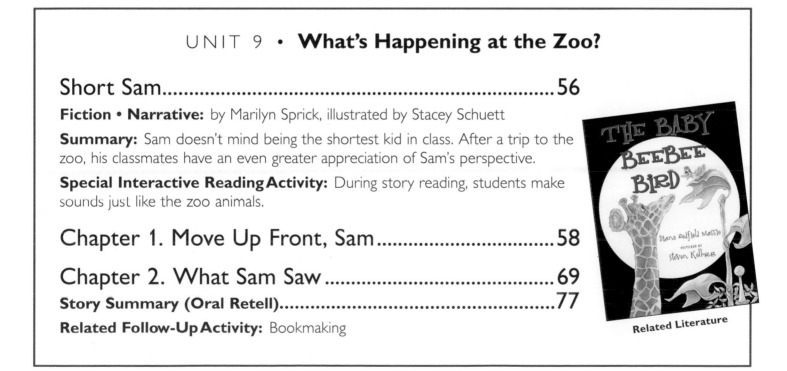

Related Literature

Related Literature

Spiders Spinning

Story 1 • Spider Facts
Story 2 • Sahale, Master Weaver

Spider Facts

INTRODUCTION

Spiders are interesting animals.
Raise your hand if you've ever seen a spider.

K–W–L (modified)

Let's make a list of things we *think* we know about spiders.
I think spiders spin webs, so I'm going to write that on the board.
What do you think you know about spiders?
Write down student responses.

We're going to read a story that tells facts about real spiders.
The title of the story is "Spider Facts."
Mrs. B wrote this story, so Mrs. B is the *author* of the story.
Who is the author? (Mrs. B)

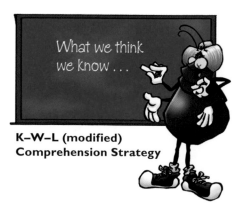

**K–W–L (modified)
Comprehension Strategy**

VOCABULARY

arachnid, ***abdomen***, ***spinneret***, ***spiderweb***
See the following pages for how to teach the vocabulary words:
arachnid (4), abdomen (9), spinneret (12), spiderweb (13).

Spider Facts

by Mrs. B

Look at the spiders on this page.

Spiders come in many shapes and sizes, but all spiders belong to a group of animals called *arachnids*.

I like that big word *arachnid*.

Everyone, say *arachnid*. (arachnid)

All spiders are the *same* because they are arachnids.
That's a fact.

Everyone, what kind of an animal is a spider? an . . . (arachnid)

All spiders are the *same* because they have eight legs.

Let's count the legs on this spider.

One, two, three, four, five, six, seven, eight.

How many legs does a spider have? (eight)

Spiders have . . . eight legs. That's another fact.

What's the same about spiders? (They have eight legs.)

What kind of animal is a spider? (an arachnid)

Look at this animal.

Let's count its legs. One, two, three, four.

This animal has . . . four legs!

Is this a spider? No!

What a silly question! Of course it isn't a spider.

Spiders have . . . (eight legs).

This animal is *not* a spider. It's an . . . elephant!

Look at this animal.

Let's count the animal's legs.

One, two.

This animal has . . .
two legs.

Is this a spider? No!

What a silly question! Of course it isn't a spider.

Spiders have . . . (eight legs).

This animal is *not* a spider. It's a . . . duck!

Look at this animal.

Let's count its legs.

One, two, three, four, five, six, seven, eight.

This animal has . . . eight legs.

Is this a spider? Yes!

This animal is a spider.

Here is another fact about spiders.

All spiders are the *same* because
they have two body parts.

How many body parts does a spider have? (two)

Together, the head and chest of the spider make one body part.

The abdomen is the other body part.

How many body parts does a spider have? (two)
The first part is the head and chest. The second part is the . . . *abdomen*.

Look at this spider.

This is the head and chest.

This is the abdomen.

Everyone, how many body parts is that? (two)

This spider has two body parts.

The first part is the head and chest. The second part is the . . . abdomen.

Look at this spider.

Let's count the body parts.
One, two.

This spider has
two body parts.

We've learned many facts about spiders.

Fact one, spiders are . . . arachnids.

Fact two, spiders have eight . . . (legs).

Fact three, spiders have two . . . (body parts).

Did you learn any other facts about a spider?
(The head and chest make one body part.
The other body part is the abdomen.)

The facts tell us what a spider is.

A *spider* is an arachnid. A spider is a small animal
with two . . . (body parts) and (eight legs).

Here is another fact about spiders.

All spiders are the *same* because they spin a silky thread from tiny spinnerets on their backs.

Everyone, look at the picture.

If you look carefully, you can see the spinnerets on this spider's back.

What do spiders spin from the spinnerets on their backs? (a silky thread)

Some spiders use the silky thread to weave beautiful webs.

Spiders spin webs in many different places.

You might find a spiderweb in a tree . . .

in the grass . .

or in the corner of your room.

Raise your hand if you've ever seen a spiderweb.

Spiderwebs can be big or small.

They can be very simple . . .
or very complex.

Spiders are very interesting!

Raise your hand if you think spiders are interesting.

PROCEED TO FACT SUMMARY

Fact Summary

Let's review the facts we learned about spiders.

Fact one, spiders are . . . (arachnids).

Fact two, spiders have eight . . . (legs).

Fact three, spiders have two . . . (body parts).

Fact four, some spiders spin . . . (webs).

Raise your hand if you can tell me other facts about spiders.
(The spider body parts are the head and chest and the abdomen.
Spiders spin silky thread from spinnerets on their backs. Spiderwebs
can be big or small. Spiderwebs can be found in many different places.)

The facts tell us what a spider is.

What is a spider? (an animal with two body parts and eight legs,
an arachnid, an animal that spins silky threads with spinnerets)

END OF STORY 1

Sahale, Master Weaver

INTRODUCTION

In our last Lap Book story, we learned that spiders are . . . arachnids.
We learned many facts about spiders.
We learned that spiders have eight . . . (legs) and two . . . (body parts).
We also learned that some spiders spin webs.

Look at the spiderweb.
Can you see the drops of water on the web?
[Daniel], please point to the drops of water.

> **VOCABULARY**
> ***dew***
>
> The little drops of water are called *dew*.
> What are the water drops called? (dew)
> In the early morning, you can often find dew on the grass.
> Close your eyes and imagine the morning dew on the
> delicate threads of a spiderweb.

This story is a made-up story about a little spider named Sahale.
You will hear many facts woven into this story about a make-believe spider.
The title of the story is "Sahale, Master Weaver."
Sahale is a an American Indian name.
The authors of the story are Barbara Gunn and Marilyn Sprick.
Bobbi Shupe drew the pictures.

Sahale,
Master Weaver

by Barbara Gunn and Marilyn Sprick

illustrated by Bobbi Shupe

Sahale was a baby spider. She was one of many babies
born in a web that hung in the window of a barn.
Sahale loved looking at the beautiful spiderwebs in
the barn, in the tall green grass, and in the apple tree.

She loved the way the sun made the delicate webs sparkle.
More than anything, Sahale wanted to spin her own webs.

Who is this story about? (a baby spider named Sahale)
At the beginning of this story, Sahale wanted to spin her own . . . (webs).

One night, Sahale dreamed of webs spun in the tall grass—webs glistening with dew in the morning sun.

What did Sahale dream of? (spiderwebs)
Sahale dreamed of spiderwebs glistening with morning . . . dew.
Close your eyes and imagine the morning dew on a spiderweb.

The morning dew is *glistening*. That means it's sparkling in the morning sun. Can you see the water drops sparkling, or glistening, in the sun?

The next morning, Sahale woke with visions of a beautiful web dancing in her head—a gorgeous web in the tall green grass. Sahale left her mother's web and crawled down the waterspout.

Everyone, look at my hands.

Here are Sahale's eight legs. This is how Sahale crawled down the waterspout.

Everyone, show me how Sahale crawled down the waterspout.

Sahale crawled through the tall green grass.

Everyone, let's make Sahale crawl through the grass with her eight legs.

The next morning when the sun came up,
all the spiders on the farm saw
that Sahale had made
a beautiful web
in the tall grass.

It was so beautiful that all the spiders clapped.

Everyone, clap for Sahale.

Sahale blushed. She was a little shy, but she smiled and bowed her head.

Everyone, smile and bow your head.

Sahale had made a beautiful web—just like the webs she had seen in her dreams. Look at the web.

Is it glistening in the morning sun?

What do you think is making it sparkle? (the morning dew)

That night, Sahale dreamed of webs spun in the apple tree.
Sahale woke the next morning with visions of a beautiful web
dancing in her head—a gorgeous web in the apple tree.

Sahale left her web
in the tall green grass.
She crawled through
the grass to the apple tree.
Then she climbed up the trunk
of the tree to the first branch.

Sahale spun a silky thread from her spinnerets and began weaving a web.

The next morning when the sun came up, all the spiders
on the farm saw that Sahale had made an even more beautiful web.
Everyone clapped. Sahale blushed. She was still a little shy,
but she smiled and bowed her head.

Everyone, smile and bow your head.

In the middle of the story, Sahale dreamed of beautiful webs and then made them.
She made one web in the . . . (grass), and she made another web in an . . . (apple tree).

That night, Sahale dreamed of webs spun in the clouds.

Sahale woke the next morning with visions of
a beautiful web dancing in her head—
a gorgeous web in the clouds.

What do you think is going to happen?

Sahale stepped from her web in the apple tree
and caught the wind.

The wind carried Sahale high into the clouds.

Everyone, show me Sahale being carried by the wind.

As she drifted through the clouds,
Sahale began spinning silver thread and weaving another web.
Sahale spun and wove all day and night.

The next morning when the sun came up,
the spiders on the farm looked up and saw
the most beautiful web they had ever seen.

Where did Sahale make the most beautiful web ever seen? (in the clouds)

For a while, the spiders were so amazed they simply stared.
Then one spider stood and began to clap.
Soon all the spiders were standing and clapping.

Everyone, stand up and clap.
Everyone, please sit down.

Sahale had woven the most beautiful web
that had ever been seen anywhere in the world.

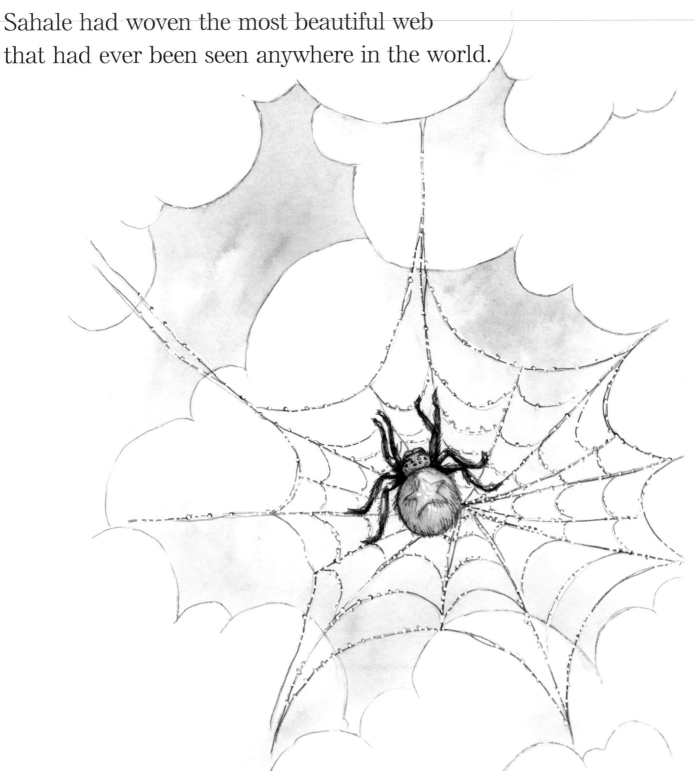

From that day on, spiders began to tell the story of Sahale,
Master Weaver. They told of her dreams and of her beautiful webs
glistening with the morning dew. Even now, little spiders love to hear
Sahale's story and dream their own dreams of weaving beautiful webs.

After Sahale made the most beautiful web ever, spiders began to tell the story of Sahale, Master . . . (Weaver).

PROCEED TO STORY SUMMARY

Story Summary

Let's retell our story.

Who is the story about? (a baby spider named Sahale)

● At the beginning of the story, Sahale wanted to spin her own . . . (webs).

■

In the middle of the story, Sahale dreamed of beautiful webs and then she made them. She made one web in the . . . (grass), and she made another web in an . . . (apple tree).

▲

At the end of the story, Sahale made the most beautiful web ever seen.
Let's describe Sahale's web. Sahale wove a beautiful web in . . . (the clouds).
The web sparkled, or . . . glistened, with the morning . . . dew.

That's when spiders began to tell the story of Sahale, Master . . . (Weaver).

READER RESPONSE:

Sahale dreamed of making beautiful webs.
Little spiders, who hear Sahale's story, dream of weaving beautiful webs.
What do you dream of?

Put one finger on your nose if you liked the story of Sahale.

END OF STORY 2

See the unit teacher's guide for related activities: Pocket Chart Retell; Bookmaking.

Worms Crawling

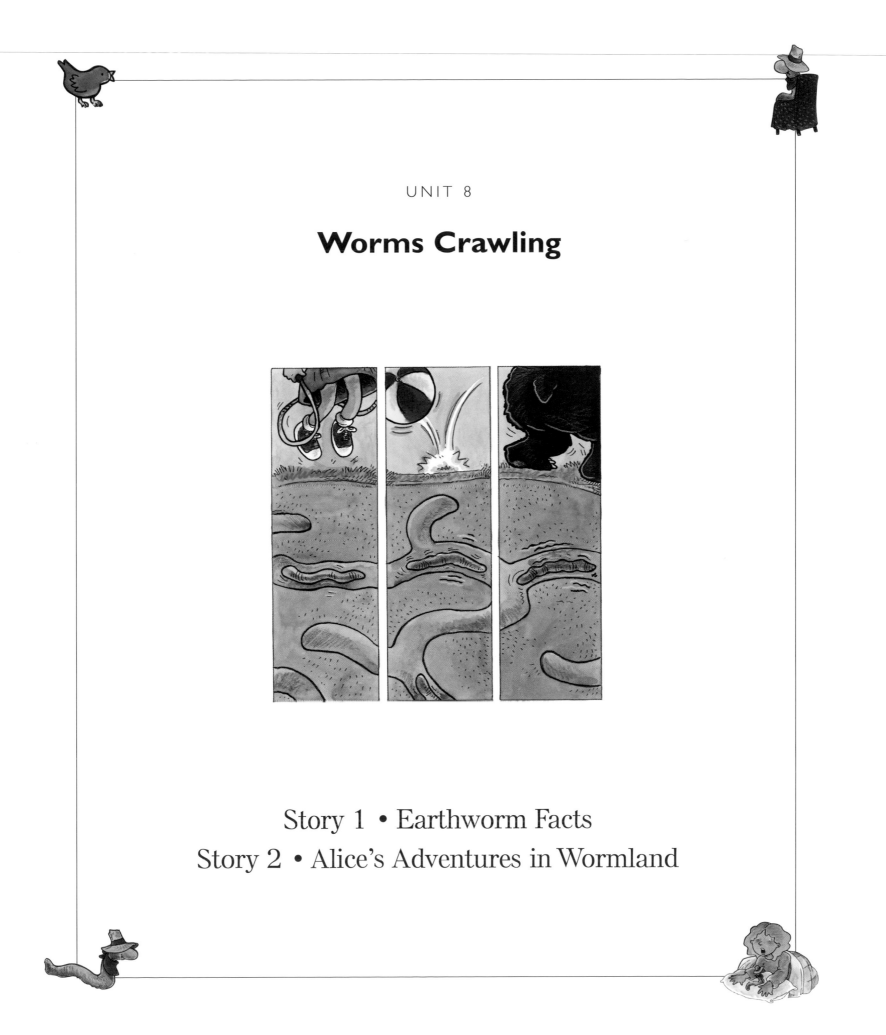

Earthworm Facts

PREPARATION

Before starting the story reading, partially fill a balloon (or balloons) with water.
The balloon(s) will be used to help children understand what a vibration
feels like.

INTRODUCTION

Earthworms are interesting animals because they have no legs and
they live underground.
Raise your hand if you've ever seen an earthworm.

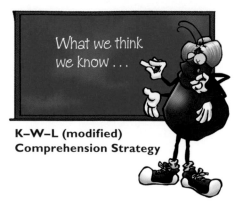

K–W–L (modified)
Let's make a list of things we think we know about earthworms.
I think earthworms dig tunnels underground, so I'll write that on the board.
What do you think you know about earthworms?
Write down student responses.

The title of our story is "Earthworm Facts." It tells facts about earthworms.
This story was written by Richard Dunn, so Richard Dunn is the . . . (author).
The person who drew the pictures is Larry Nolte.

K–W–L (modified)
Comprehension Strategy

Earthworm Facts

by Richard Dunn

illustrated by Larry Nolte

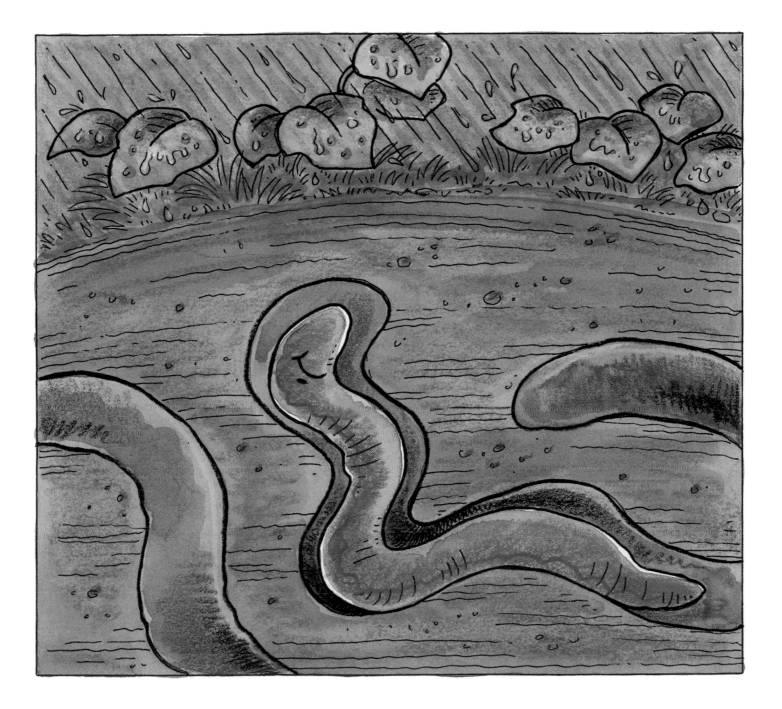

Earthworms don't have eyes.

If you were an earthworm, this is what you would see.

What a funny picture!
There's nothing in it because earthworms don't have . . . (eyes).
Everyone, what do you think earthworms see? (nothing)

Here is a fact about earthworms. Earthworms don't have eyes.

Earthworms can't see anything. That's another . . . fact.

Earthworms don't have ears, but their body has special parts to help them feel things move. If you were an earthworm, you would feel *vibrations* in the ground.

Vibrations. That's a great word. Everyone say *vibrations.* (vibrations)

I've made a water balloon.
When I hold the water balloon in the palm of my hand and give it a firm tap, it vibrates, or moves.

Who would like to feel the vibration?

Can you feel the balloon move?

Everyone, that's called a . . . vibration.

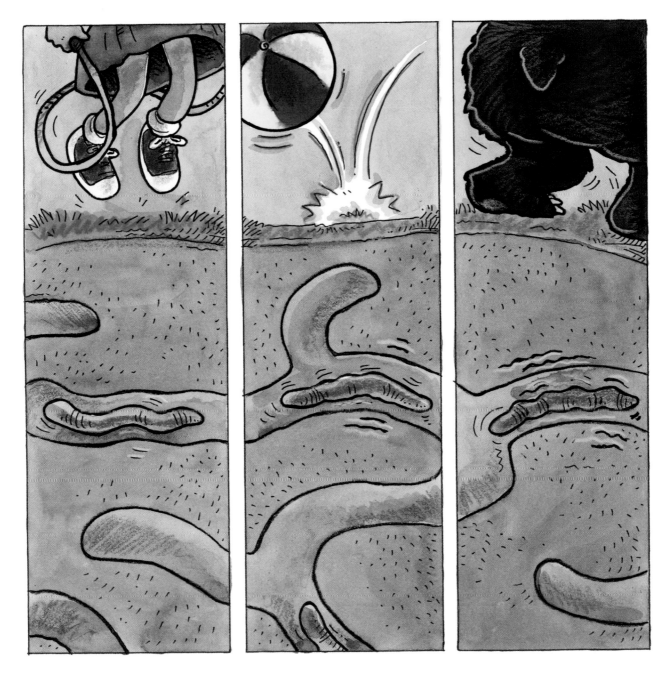

Let's look at these three pictures.
What do you see?

Earthworms can feel vibrations in the ground. If you were an earthworm, you would feel vibrations below the ground.

Touch your nose. Now take a deep breath through your nose.

Do you think earthworms have a nose?

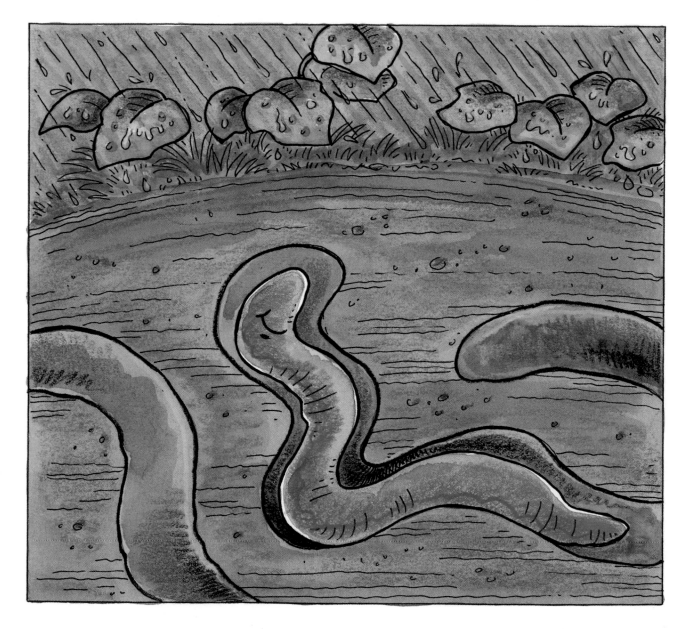

Earthworms don't have a nose. If you were an earthworm, you would breathe through your skin.

How do earthworms breathe? (through their skin)

Yes, earthworms breathe through their skin. That's a fact.

Some people think earthworms are slimy, but earthworms cannot breathe if their skin becomes dry. If you were an earthworm, you would be glad that you were slimy!

Earthworms don't have eyes, or ears, or a nose, but they do have a mouth. They use their mouth to eat dead leaves and other things in the dirt.

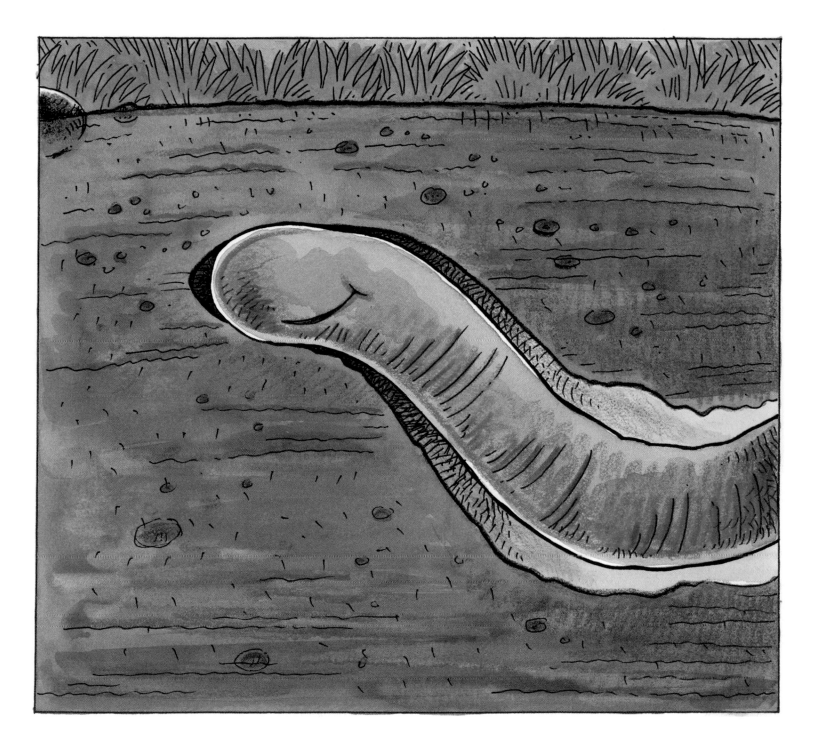

Everyone, touch your eyes. Do earthworms have eyes? (no)
Everyone, touch your ears. Do earthworms have ears? (no)
Everyone, touch your nose. Do earthworms have a nose? (no)
Everyone, touch your mouth. Do earthworms have a mouth? (yes)
What do earthworms feel underground when something moves? (vibrations)

Here's another fact about earthworms. They are helpful to gardeners. Earthworms dig tunnels that make the dirt soft, so the roots of plants can grow. This helps the plants grow strong and healthy.

How do earthworms help plants grow? (They make the dirt soft, so the roots of plants can grow.)

Earthworms are very interesting animals!

PROCEED TO FACT SUMMARY

Fact Summary

Let's review the facts we learned about earthworms.

We learned that earthworms . . .

    (have no eyes)

    (can't see)

    (have no ears)

    (can't hear)

    (feel vibrations)

Raise your hand if you can tell me other facts about earthworms.
(Earthworms don't have a nose.
Earthworms breathe through their skin.
Earthworms do have a mouth.
Earthworms dig tunnels.
Earthworms help plants grow by making the dirt soft.)

END OF STORY 1

Alice's Adventures in Wormland

INTRODUCTION

In our last story, we learned facts about earthworms.
Our story today is about a girl who has an interesting
dream about earthworms.
The title of the story is "Alice's Adventures in Wormland."
The authors are Barbara Gunn and Marilyn Sprick.
Who are the authors? (Barbara Gunn and Marilyn Sprick)
Larry Nolte drew the pictures for this story.

Alice's Adventures in Wormland

by Barbara Gunn and Marilyn Sprick

illustrated by Larry Nolte

Alice's class had been studying earthworms at school. Most of the children in Alice's class thought earthworms were cool, but Alice didn't really like them. That all changed one night when Alice dreamed a most unusual dream.

Who is this story about? (a girl named Alice)

How does Alice feel about earthworms? (She doesn't really like them.)

But that changes when Alice dreams. I wonder what Alice is going to dream about.

What do you think?

Alice had fallen into a deep sleep.

Everyone, this is Alice sleeping.

Show me with your hands, arms, and eyes what Alice is doing.

In her dream, Alice sat up and looked around. The pictures on her wall were nowhere to be seen. Her dresser had disappeared too. She was in a tunnel surrounded by dirt.

Alice cried, "Oh my!"

Just then, Alice heard a little voice. A small worm sat on her bed. The small worm wore a pretty little yellow gardening hat and a purple scarf.

"Oh my!" cried Alice. "What are you doing on my bed?"

"My name is Tierra," the little worm said. "You and your bed are in my tunnel."

Alice looked around.
She was so embarrassed. "I'm sorry," said Alice.
"I don't know how my bed and I got in your tunnel."

When Alice went to sleep, she had a dream.
In her dream, Alice found herself in a dirt tunnel talking to a . . . (worm).

Tierra was a sweet worm, so she said, "It's no bother. You and your bed are welcome in my tunnel. Would you like to join me for a cup of tea?"

Alice said, "Thank you. A cup of tea sounds like just the right thing."

"Follow me," said Tierra. Then off she went digging a tunnel under the ground. Alice followed on her hands and knees.

Everyone, show me how Alice crawled through the tunnel on her hands and knees.

Now, go back quietly to your place.

Before she knew it, Alice was sitting in a large, comfy chair in a corner of Tierra's lovely burrow. The walls were made of damp earth, and roots hung from the ceiling.

Where are Alice and Tierra? (in Tierra's burrow)

A *burrow* is a hole dug in the ground. A burrow is an animal's underground home.

What is a burrow? (an underground home)

The two new friends sat quietly sipping their tea and chatting.

Alice and Tierra had become . . . (friends).

After a bit, Alice said, "We learned in school that earthworms have no eyes."

Tierra said, "Wow! You are studying worms. I'm honored." Then Tierra tipped her yellow hat a bit, and Alice could see that Tierra had no eyes.

Everyone, did Tierra have eyes? (no)

Why not? (She is a worm.)

Suddenly Tierra asked,
"Can you feel that?"

Alice said, "Feel what?"

"That vibration," answered Tierra.

"Vibration?" said Alice.
"Oh, I remember. We learned that big word in school. Our teacher told us that you can feel vibrations."

Tierra said, "If you sit very quietly and put your hand on the ground, you will be able to feel the ground move."

Alice put her hand on the ground. She said, "Oh my! It feels like thunder in the ground."

"That's your mother walking above us in her garden," said Tierra.

"Oh, my!" said Alice.

Everyone, what did Alice feel? (a vibration)
Yes, Alice was able to feel the ground . . . move.

49

"What else did you learn about us in school?" asked Tierra.

Alice said, "We learned that you are gardeners."

"Really?" said Tierra. "I've never planted a garden."

Alice said, "Not like that. You eat dead leaves and make the dirt very rich."

Then Alice said, "We also learned that your digging makes the soil soft and airy. The roots of our plants like that."

"Wow!" said Tierra. "I didn't know we were so important."

"You are," said Alice, and she really meant it.

Alice explained to Tierra how worms were . . . (important).

How do earthworms help plants grow? (They make the dirt rich. They make the dirt soft and airy.)

Just then, Alice thought she heard her mother calling. When she looked around, she was back in her own room. She rubbed her eyes. The soft brown dirt was gone. The pictures were on the wall. The dresser was in the corner, and the sun was shining through the window.

Is Alice still dreaming? (no)

Alice said, "Oh my! What a dream I had!"

Everyone, what did Alice say? (Oh my! What a dream I had!)

Alice spent the rest of the day helping her mom plant seedlings in the garden. As Alice dug in the soft brown dirt, she imagined Tierra busily tunneling below.

She also started thinking about the next story she would write at school. It would be about a little worm who wore a yellow hat and a purple scarf.

What did Alice do after she woke up? (helped her mom in the garden; thought about writing a story)

How do you think Alice feels about earthworms now?

PROCEED TO STORY SUMMARY

Story Summary

Let's retell our story.

Who is this story about? (a girl named Alice)

● At the beginning of the story, Alice didn't like earthworms.

Then she had a dream about a . . . (worm named Tierra).

■

In the middle of the story, Alice dreamed she was with Tierra in Tierra's burrow.
They were having tea and chatting. They had become . . . (friends).

At the end of the story, Alice woke up. Then she helped her mom in the . . . (garden) and thought about writing a . . . (story).

READER RESPONSE:

Alice didn't like earthworms at the beginning of the story, but she changed her mind after she met Tierra in her dream.

How do you feel about earthworms?

END OF STORY 2

See the unit teacher's guide for related activities: Pocket Chart Retell; Bookmaking.

What's Happening at the Zoo?

Short Sam

Short Sam

INTRODUCTION

The title of this story is "Short Sam."
Everyone, what is the title of the story? (Short Sam)
The story is by Marilyn Sprick. Who is the author? (Marilyn Sprick)
The person who drew the pictures is Stacey Schuett.

VOCABULARY

zoo

See page 61 for how to teach the vocabulary word "zoo."

Note: Read Well periodically uses easy words like "zoo" to help
students learn the language of definitions. With the word "zoo,"
students define a place. A *zoo* is a place where people can go
to see animals.

Short Sam

by Marilyn Sprick

illustrated by Stacey Schuett

Chapter 1

Move Up Front, Sam

Some children are tall, and some are short. Some children have curly hair, and others have straight hair. Some children are bouncy, and others are still. Some children are loud, and others are quiet.

Sam has red hair, freckles, no front teeth, and a great big smile.
Sam is also the shortest kid in his class, but he doesn't mind.

Everyone, who is this story about? (Sam)

What are some things we know about Sam?
(He has red hair, freckles, no front teeth, and a great big smile. He is short.)

Does Sam mind being short? (no)

No, Sam doesn't mind being short. He always has a great big smile, and that's what people remember about him.

Sam is everyone's best friend.

What is special about Sam? (He is everyone's best friend.)

One day, Sam's teacher, Mr. Jackson, announced,
"Next Monday morning we're going to the zoo!"

All the children cheered. Sam smiled his great big smile.

Everyone, show me a great big smile.

At the beginning of the story, Sam and his class found out they were going to go to the . . . (zoo).

What is a zoo?

Yes, a zoo is a place where people can go to see animals. Many of the animals are from faraway places.
What are some animals that you might see in a zoo?

During the week before the trip, the class learned how to draw
zoo animals.

Mr. Jackson said that after their trip they would make books about
what they saw at the zoo.

What did the class learn to do? (draw animals)
Their teacher told them they would make zoo . . . (books).

They learned how to draw elephants, hyenas, lions, tigers, giraffes, and apes.

What animals do you think the kids might see at the zoo?

When the day of the trip finally arrived, everyone was really excited!

At the zoo, the first stop was the Big Elephant House—where the children could hear the elephants trumpeting.

When elephants trumpet, they make loud noises that sound like a horn. Everyone, pretend your arm is an elephant's trunk. Now make a noise like an elephant trumpeting.

Sam was at the back of the crowd and couldn't see *anything*.

Why couldn't Sam see anything? (He was too short to see over the other kids.)
What do you think Sam should do?

Sam started jumping up and down.

Mr. Jackson saw him and said, "Children, Sam can't see. Please let him move up."

When Sam got up to the front, he smiled his great big smile.

Everyone, show me a great big smile.

The next stop was the Lions' Den, where the children could see and hear the big cats roaring.

Sam was at the back again, and he couldn't see *anything*.

So Sam said, in as loud a voice as he could, "I can't see."

What did Sam say? (I can't see.)

The other kids said, "Come on Sam, move up front."

Were the other kids nice to Sam? (yes) Why?

When Sam got to the front, he yelled, "Thank you!" He had to yell because the lions were making such a ruckus.

What did Sam yell? (thank you)

Sam wasn't sure if the kids could hear him, so he also smiled his great big smile.

Show me a big smile. Sam is a nice kid. He always appreciates his friends.

By the time the class got to the Hyenas' Den, Sam was once again in the back. He couldn't see *anything*, but he could hear the hyenas howling.

Hyenas are like wild dogs. Make a sound that you think a wild dog or hyena would make.

This time Sam crawled through the tangle of legs and tennis shoes to get to the front. When he got there, Sam again flashed his great big smile at all the kids.

Sam and his class are at the zoo. What is a zoo? (a place where people go to see animals)

Sam couldn't see the animals because he was always at the . . . (back).

Then he would move up to the . . . (front) so he could . . . (see).

Sam and his class had a great morning at the zoo. They saw a lot of big exotic animals from all over the world. They saw elephants, hyenas, lions, tigers, giraffes, and apes.

Soon it was time to get back to school.

What do you think the kids liked seeing the most?

END OF CHAPTER 1

Short Sam

CHAPTER 2 INTRODUCTION

We've read Chapter 1 of "Short Sam."
Who is the story about? (a boy named Sam)
What are some things we know about Sam? (He has red hair. He has freckles.
He smiles a great big smile. He's the shortest kid in his class.)

In Chapter 1, Sam and his class found out they were going to the . . . (zoo).
What is a zoo? (a place where people go to see animals)
What animals did the kids see at the zoo? (elephants, lions, hyenas, tigers . . .)
At the end of the chapter, Sam and his class were on their way back to school.

VOCABULARY
unique
See page 73 for how to teach the vocabulary word "unique."

Chapter 2

What Sam Saw

After Sam and his class got back to school, they began to make their zoo books. Mr. Jackson reminded the children that their books should include pictures of things they had seen at the zoo.

The class spent a very busy afternoon drawing, cutting, and gluing.

Sam seemed the busiest of all.

What did the class do when they got back to school? (made zoo books)

Shortly before it was time to go home, Mr. Jackson
gathered the children together for circle time.
He told them to bring their zoo
books to share.

James went first. This is what James drew.

What had James seen?
(an elephant)

Mr. Jackson said, "James, that's a great picture. Elephants come from
faraway places. A zoo is one of the few places you can see an elephant."
James smiled and everyone clapped for him. Then the class chanted,
"We went to the zoo. We went to the zoo. We all saw the elephants too!"

Everyone, what did the children chant? (We went to the zoo . . .)

Grace went next. This is what Grace drew.

What had Grace seen? (a lion)

Mr. Jackson said, "Nice job, Grace. A zoo is one of the few places you can see a lion." Grace smiled. Everyone clapped for Grace. Then the class chanted, "We went to the zoo. We went to the zoo. We all saw the lion too!"

What did the children chant? (We went to the zoo. We went . . .)

Esmeralda went next.
This is what Esmeralda drew.

What had Esmeralda seen? (a giraffe)

Mr. Jackson said, "That's a wonderful giraffe. A zoo is one of the few places you can see a giraffe." Everyone clapped for Esmeralda. Then the class chanted, "We went to the zoo. We went to the zoo. We all saw the giraffe too!"

What did the children chant? (We went to the zoo. We went . . .)

Where would we go to see a giraffe? (a zoo)

Why wouldn't you see a giraffe in your neighborhood?

Finally, it was Sam's turn.

Sam smiled and showed
everyone his first page.
This is what Sam drew.

What had Sam seen? (a spider)

At first, everyone was quiet.

Why was everyone quiet?

Then Alex said, "You saw a spider! How cool! Where'd you see that spider?"

Sam said, "It was on the railing at the Big Elephant House.
Didn't you see it? It was big and hairy, and it had eight legs."

No one else had seen the spider. Sam's picture was unique.

Unique means that it was one of a kind.
Why do you think no one else had seen the spider?

Mr. Jackson said, "Sam, what do you have on your next page?"

Sam smiled his great big smile.

Sam had drawn ants.

What else had Sam seen? (ants)

Cassie said, "Where'd you see the ants?"

Sam said, "At the Lions' Den. There was a whole parade of ants marching through the melted chocolate. Didn't you see them? They were awesome!"

Mr. Jackson said, "This page is great Sam. It is unique."

Why was Sam's picture unique, or one of a kind? (Sam was the only one who drew ants.)
Why do you think no one else saw the ants?

Mr. Jackson smiled at Sam and said, "Sam, what do you have on your next page? Is it also unique?"

Sam's smile stretched from ear to ear.

This is what Sam drew.

What else had Sam seen?
(a mosquito)
Was Sam's picture of the mosquito unique?
Why?

Tamela leaned over and scratched her leg.

Why do you think Tamela is scratching her leg?

Tamela said, "I saw one tiger, two lions, three hyenas, four elephants, five giraffes, and six apes. But I missed the spider, the ants, *and* the mosquito. Mr. Jackson, don't you think we should go back to the zoo so we can see them too?"

Mr. Jackson said, "What do you think, class?"

Sam and the class smiled and cheered.

Mr. Jackson said, "I would like to see the spider and the ants, but I don't think I want to see the mosquito." Then Mr. Jackson reached over and scratched his knee.

Why do you think Mr. Jackson doesn't want to see the mosquito again?

Sam reached over and scratched his knee too.

He'd had a great day and so had the mosquito.

PROCEED TO STORY SUMMARY

Story Summary

Let's retell our story.

Who is this story about? (a boy named Sam)

Tell me about Sam. (He has red hair, freckles, and a big smile.
He's the shortest one in his class.)

Was it a problem for Sam to be short? (no)

Why not? (He had a big smile and was everyone's best friend.)

● At the beginning of the story, Sam and his class found
out they were going to the . . . (zoo).

They learned to draw . . . (animals) because afterward
they would make zoo . . . (books).

■ In the middle of the story, Sam and his class were at
the zoo.

Sam couldn't see anything because he was always at
the . . . (back).

Then he would move up to the . . . (front) so he
could . . . (see).

 **Bobbi Shupe** is a Colorado native and has a tremendous love for the Rocky Mountains. She enjoys hiking and backpacking but would rather spend time on the river bank sketching than actually fishing. Bobbi does freelance design and illustration through her own company—specializing in children's illustration from fabric design to book covers and interiors.

Larry Nolte doodles for a living. He has published several children's books, which together are taller than a stack of pancakes. He lives on the south side of St. Louis in an old "arts and crafts" style house with his lovely wife, three wonderful children, and a most unique dog.

 **Stacey Schuett** was a dreamy kid who loved to make things up . . . stories, pictures, and past lives. She lives in Northern California with her partner, Lesly; their two children, Clare and Ian; two parakeets, a cat, a rabbit, a dog, and a part-time visiting tarantula. To date, she has illustrated more than 25 children's books and written a few. Even though she's not a little kid anymore, most days, she still gets to do what she likes best—stare out the window and make stuff up.